The Great BEaR ReScue

Saving the Gobi Bears

Sandra Markle

M Millbrook Press • Minneapolis

For Alicia Bashawaty and the children of Kennedy Elementary School in Livonia, Michigan

Acknowledgments: The author would like to thank the following people for sharing their enthusiasm and expertise: Derek Craighead, founder, president, and executive director of Craighead Beringia South, Kelly, Wyoming; Dr. Janet Hawkes, consultant to Great Green Partners and Food for Mazaalai; Dr. Michael Proctor, Birchdale Ecological, & International Association for Bear Research and Management, Kaslo, BC, Canada; Dr. Harry Reynolds, Gobi Bear Project, founder; Gobi Bear Fund, Fairbanks, Alaska; and Odbayar Tumendemberel, University of South-Eastern Norway, Telemark, Norway.

A special thank-you to Skip Jeffery for his loving support during the creative process.

Millbrook Press™
An imprint of Lerner Publishing Group, Inc.
241 First Avenue North
Minneapolis, MN 55401 USA

For reading levels and more information, look up this title at www.lernerbooks.com.

Main body text set in Metro Office. Typeface provided by Linotype AG.

Library of Congress Cataloging-in-Publication Data

Names: Markle, Sandra, author.
Title: The great bear rescue : saving the Gobi bears / Sandra Markle.
Description: Minneapolis : Millbrook Press, [2021] | Series: Sandra Markle's science discoveries | Includes bibliographical references and index. | Audience: Ages 8–14 | Audience: Grades 4–6 | Summary: "This fascinating look at Gobi bears—the rarest bears on the planet—includes the story of why so few of these bears remain and what scientists are doing to help this critically endangered species" —Provided by publisher.
Identifiers: LCCN 2019051392 (print) | LCCN 2019051393 (ebook) | ISBN 9781541581258 (library binding) | ISBN 9781728401553 (ebook)
Subjects: LCSH: Brown bear—Conservation—Gobi Desert (Mongolia and China)—Juvenile literature.
Classification: LCC QL737.C27 M3216 2021 (print) | LCC QL737.C27 (ebook) | DDC 333.95/9784095173—dc23

LC record available at https://lccn.loc.gov/2019051392
LC ebook record available at https://lccn.loc.gov/2019051393

Manufactured in the United States of America
1-47324-47951-2/21/2020

TABLE OF CONTENTS

Gobi bears have an extra-thick fur coat to protect them against the desert heat and cold.

IS IT SAFE?

It's late October in Mongolia's Gobi Desert, and the chill wind is a reminder that winter is coming. The female Gobi bear's instincts tell her it's nearly time to hibernate. So she stops by each wild rhubarb plant she finds to dig up the starchy roots to eat. This is exactly the food she needs to finish fattening up before she sleeps away the winter. But the wind is carrying another scent that makes her stop. She lifts her big head, sniffs, and then moves on, following her nose to track the new scent—water.

In her world, the vast Gobi Desert, drinking her fill of water means either staying close to an oasis for water or traveling from one oasis to another. Because food is in short supply in any one spot, the Gobi bear can't just stay near one oasis. She must keep moving to find enough food. But now with the lure of water so close, she picks up her pace until the wind shifts again and delivers a new scent.

She smells *people*. The bear hesitates—but only for a few seconds. Her thirst is an ache, and the water scent is stronger than the human scent. She plods on, cautiously approaching the oasis.

When she rounds a rock outcropping, she sees a group of people straight ahead. They're clustered around something else she fears—fire. She stops. One of the people makes a loud noise, and the whole group rears up. They're facing her. The Gobi bear huffs a throaty growl, but the water scent is strong and her thirst is great. So she doesn't run.

Will the people attack her? Or will they let her get to the water?

GOBI BEARS IN TROUBLE

This female has to survive! Bear researchers believe that fewer than forty Gobi bears are left in the world. So why are these bears in trouble? And what's the big deal?

The big deal is Gobi bears are unique. They are the only bears in the world to live entirely in a desert habitat. They're found only in the Gobi Desert, which stretches across southern Mongolia and northern China. Mongolian people consider them a national treasure. But living in only one place—a very difficult place to live—is also why the Gobi bear population is in trouble.

The Gobi Desert is dry because rain from the Indian Ocean to the south is blocked by Earth's highest mountains, the Himalayas. Rainstorms from the Pacific Ocean to the east dump most of their water on China, the Korean Peninsula, and Japan, leaving little to reach the Gobi Desert.

The other big deal is that Gobi bears are what scientists call an *umbrella species*. That means what the bears need to survive also covers the needs of other animals sharing their habitat. If conservation efforts can help Gobi bears get the food and water they need, a number of other endangered Gobi Desert animals would be likely to survive too.

So helping the Gobi bears would also help multiple other animals, including Bactrian camels, black-tailed gazelles, snow leopards, and Przewalski's horses.

Przewalski's horses were once nearly extinct—no more of them would exist. They were raised in protected areas and reintroduced to the desert. They are still listed as endangered, facing a high risk of extinction.

Long ago, Gobi bears roamed the steppes, the grasslands rimming the Gobi Desert. Nomadic Mongolian herders also brought their goats, sheep, and camels there to graze. By the mid-1900s, competition for food pushed the Gobi bears from the steppes into the desert, and amazingly, the bears adapted to living in this harsh habitat.

Harry Reynolds, a researcher who studies brown bears, said, "Today, they are unique among the eight species of bears and dwell exclusively in a desert habitat. By adaptation and learning, they've found a way to live in one of the most extreme environments on the planet."

Although Gobi bears occasionally eat insects and mouselike jerboas, they're mainly vegetarians. Their favorite foods are wild rhubarb rhizomes (the rootlike parts that store food for the plant), nitre bush berries, and wild onions, which are native to the parts of the Gobi Desert where they live.

A scientist examines a sedated Gobi bear and sees that digging roots has worn down the bear's claws.

Gobi bears mainly eat wild rhubarb rhizomes.

What and Where Is the Gobi Desert?

The Gobi Desert is Earth's fifth-largest desert. In Mongolian, Gobi means "waterless place," and the desert is that. While this desert can get as much as 8 inches (20 cm) of rain a year, most years it receives less. In drought years, less than a half inch (1.2 cm) of precipitation may fall where the bears live, or it might not rain at all. And conditions are getting worse because of climate change, or major long-term changes in weather patterns all over the world. A 2016 report on climate change revealed the Gobi Desert is one of Earth's most rapidly warming regions. Droughts are expected to last even longer than usual in the future. That is likely to make already difficult living conditions worse for Gobi bears.

The Gobi Desert environment is extreme: summer temperatures climb as high as 113°F (45°C), and winter temperatures drop as low as –40°F (–40°C). Bactrian camels are also at home there.

Meet the Gobi Bears

Gobi bears are most closely related to grizzly bears. Both are brown bears. Check out the features that make Gobi bears different.

Size: Adult Gobi bears are about 1 foot (0.3 m) shorter and have much lighter fur than most adult grizzlies have. Males are bigger than females, but adult male Gobi bears only weigh about 200 to 350 pounds (90 to 160 kg), while male grizzly bears with access to high-calorie foods like salmon may weigh up to 1,700 pounds (770 kg).

Diet: Gobi bears mainly eat plants. Grizzlies eat both plants and animals—even big prey, such as elk or moose.

Physical traits: Gobi bears have thick winter coats, including a much thicker undercoat than grizzlies. This helps them survive the winter. Gobi bears can only dig so far into the dry soil, so they usually hibernate where they are only partially sheltered—in a shallow hole in a hillside or only slightly covered by brush. But grizzlies are completely sheltered when they hibernate.

Gobi bears are what scientists call an *ecotype*, an animal uniquely adapted to survive in its environment.

HOME SWEET PROTECTED AREA

The Mongolian government knew it had to do something to help its national treasure. In 1953 Mongolia banned hunting Gobi bears, but that wasn't enough to help the bear population rebound. So in 1976, the Mongolian government set aside the part of the Gobi Desert where the bears were known to roam as restricted land. The goal was to stop, or at least discourage, people from grazing their herds in the area. Named the Great Gobi Strictly Protected Area (GGSPA), this includes more than 17,900 square miles (46,400 sq. km) of desert or semiarid grassland. The government hoped this would help the Gobi bear population recover.

The Great Gobi Strictly Protected Area (GGSPA) is the fourteenth-largest protected area in the world. A little over five times the size of Yellowstone National Park in the United States, it has two parts: GGSPA(A) is where the Gobi bears live, and GGSPA(B) is mainly habitat for black-tailed gazelles and Przewalski's horses.

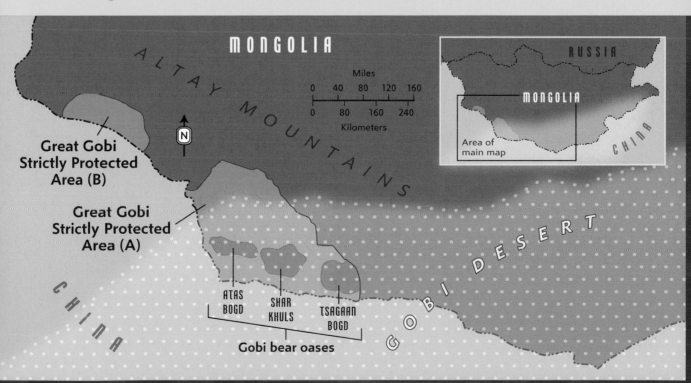

MONGOLIA

ALTAY MOUNTAINS

Great Gobi Strictly Protected Area (B)

Great Gobi Strictly Protected Area (A)

ATAS BOGD

SHAR KHULS

TSAGAAN BOGD

Gobi bear oases

GOBI DESERT

CHINA

Miles
0 40 80 120 160

0 80 160 240
Kilometers

RUSSIA

MONGOLIA

Area of main map

CHINA

Since 1987 Gobi bears have been included in Mongolia's list of endangered native species. While this list is based on the standards the International Union for Conservation of Nature (IUCN) uses for its Red List to determine if a species is in trouble, it's only for the bear's home country. Gobi bears haven't yet been classified by the IUCN as a separate species of bear. Yet recognizing Gobi bears need help was an important step toward launching conservation efforts on their behalf. The Zoological Society of London also recognized the Gobi bear as being in trouble. Both organizations list them as critically endangered (facing an extremely high risk of extinction) because scientists estimated that as few as forty Gobi bears remained anywhere. And no Gobi bears were in zoos to maintain the species.

Saving Gobi bears had become a conservation emergency. So the Mongolian government brought experts from around the world together to explore ways to save Gobi bears from extinction. Harry Reynolds was one of them.

Why, Harry wondered, was this bear, which had so perfectly adapted to its extreme environment, on the brink of disappearing? He knew it was important to find out.

In the early 1970s, wells were drilled to supply sheep, goat, and camel herds with water. Unfortunately, this led to herds grazing in one place for much longer periods. So the amount of plant food available for both the livestock and the bears dramatically decreased.

The GGSPA needed to be large so there would be room for the Gobi bears to find food, water, and mates.

In 2005 the Mongolian government invited Harry, as president of the International Association for Bear Research and Management, to form the Gobi Bear Project. This group of experts from Mongolia and around the world had some big goals. They wanted to estimate the remaining number of Gobi bears and determine how to prevent the bears from becoming extinct. They also wanted to help the population recover and increase.

Since neither the hunting ban nor having a protected habitat had helped the Gobi bear population rebound, the big question was, What would help the bears survive?

TRACKING DOWN CLUES

The scientists with the Gobi Bear Project needed to learn more about the bears. As Derek Craighead, one of the researchers, said, "Anything we could learn would be valuable because almost nothing was known about Gobi bears."

The researchers needed to capture and examine some of the bears. During a drought in the early 1990s, when food was scarce, the Mongolian government had built bear-feeding stations near oases in the GGSPA. These feeding stations would be the easiest place to catch Gobi bears. Harry's team put special bear treats, such as raisins and jam, inside a cage near a feeding station. A bear entering triggered the cage door, shutting it. Next, Harry jabbed the trapped bear with a tranquilizer dart through an opening in the cage. The team removed the sleeping bear from the cage, checked to see if it was male or female, and weighed and measured it. They also collected tissue and blood samples to check for diseases and to help with the genetic studies.

Harry Reynolds (*left*) and Michael Proctor (*right*) check the wear on a bear's teeth to know if the bear is old or young.

The Gobi Bear Project team weighs a sedated bear. Its weight offers an important insight into how well the bear is eating.

Before the bear woke up, the team placed a GPS tracking collar around the bear's neck. The collar's number was recorded along with the bear's ID, usually a number. A few bears were given names, such as Mother, Manduhai (after a Mongolian queen), Borte (after Genghis Khan's queen), and Altan (Mongolian for "golden").

Once a sedated bear woke up and left the feeding station, satellite transmissions let the scientists track and record its travels.

The researchers did this work in April or May, as the bears emerged hungry from hibernation and went to the feeding stations. For about the next fourteen months, the team collected GPS locations at least a few times a day for each collared bear.

The GPS Tracking Collar

The Gobi Bear Project used a GPS tracking collar made of rubberized nylon so it was flexible and durable. It could be programmed to transmit the bear's precise location every twenty minutes, every hour, or even every three days. Because the collars didn't need to transmit while the bear was hibernating, the collars were programmed to transmit rarely during the winter months. With frequent reporting, the battery power was used up in about three months. With less frequent transmissions, the collar could keep transmitting for fourteen months. A fall-off trigger would let scientists know the collar had fallen off. With any luck, scientists would recover the collar at its last-reported location, give it a fresh battery the following year, reprogram it, and reuse it.

A Gobi bear wears a GPS tracking collar, which weighs only 28 ounces (793 g)—a little more than a basketball.

The researchers soon learned that the bears they were capturing needed more food. The bears were too thin in August and September before they began to hibernate. They were so thin that they probably wouldn't have enough stored-up body fat to be healthy when they finished hibernating in the spring.

If a bear was pregnant, she would have an even greater need for stored body fat. Harry said, "Having a fat reserve is extremely important for expectant mothers because without it they may not be able to give birth during the winter as bears do—or nurse their young until they emerge from their dens [and start feeding again] in March or April." The only way the bear population could grow would be for mothers to give birth to healthy cubs.

This young Gobi bear needs to eat all it can to stay healthy and grow.

It's a Gobi Bear's Life

Gobi bears usually mate in June, but the developing young stops growing after just ten days. That way, the mother can put all her food energy from eating during the summer and fall into building up fat reserves for the winter.

In November a pregnant female finds a protected site to hibernate. Early in December, the cub begins to develop again. But this only happens if the mother has enough fat reserves to provide for her own body's needs plus that of the developing young. Otherwise, the young stops growing, and the pregnancy ends. If the developing young continues to grow, the mother wakes up long enough to give birth about two months later. At first, the cub is no bigger than a can of soup and its eyes are sealed shut. It also has no teeth, and its hair is too short to keep it warm. The cub snuggles against its mother for warmth, wiggles until it finds a nipple, and nurses. It continues to nurse and grow for the rest of the winter. By the time the mother and cub emerge in the spring, the cub's eyes are open, it has teeth and a fuzzy coat, and it weighs about 17 pounds (8 kg).

This Gobi bear cub, hunting for food with its mother, is learning that a feeding station can be a source of food.

The food provided at the feeding stations is dry grain pellets similar to the food farmers feed cattle and sheep.

Starting in 2005, the Gobi Bear Project team worked to build even more bear-feeding stations near oases in the GGSPA. They stocked the feeding stations in August and September, the time the bears needed to fatten up for hibernation.

By the spring of 2006, the Gobi Bear Project team realized that providing food in the fall wasn't enough. With the desert conditions drier than ever, plants the bears counted on eating when they woke up were slower to start their springtime growth. So the feeding stations were stocked again in March and April.

But the bears needed more than food for their survival. Fortunately, the land chosen for the GGSPA had been set aside because it offered something else absolutely critical for their survival—water.

In rainy times, each oasis complex offers plenty of water. In dry times, the entire complex may be reduced to a single small pond.

The GGSPA supplied the bears with year-round sources of water at three main oasis complexes: Atas Bogd, Shar Khuls, and Tsagaan Bogd. Each complex includes from seven to fourteen water sources during rainy periods. The largest water source, in Shar Khuls, flows through a half-mile-wide (0.8 km), 2-mile-long (3.2 km) valley before disappearing into the dry desert. The second largest, within Tsagaan Bogd, is just 20 feet (6 m) wide and flows for only a quarter mile (0.4 km) before vanishing into the desert. Most of the rest of the water sources at all three oasis complexes are small ponds, just a few feet in diameter.

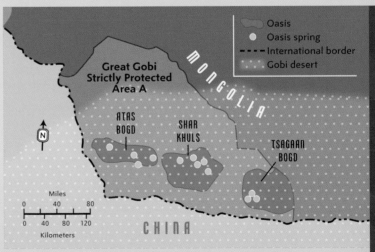

Each of the three main oasis complexes is separated by as much as 62 miles (100 km) of dry Gobi Desert terrain.

Before they can live on their own, bear cubs need at least a couple of years with their mothers. Their mothers teach them what to eat and where to find food and water in different seasons.

In 2005, during some of the brainstorming sessions for how to help the Gobi bear population survive, Mongolian officials proposed launching a captive breeding program in zoos. Then later, the captive-bred bears could be reintroduced to the Gobi Desert. This had worked for saving Mongolia's wild Przewalski's horses when they were on the brink of extinction. But horse colts can quickly survive on their own, while bear cubs need more time to roam their desert habitat with their mothers. With water and food resources so scattered, the cubs need to experience finding these critical supplies. "Besides," Harry said, "starting a captive breeding program would mean taking some females away from their natural habitat, and risk pushing the already incredibly small breeding population to the brink [of extinction]."

Since the Gobi Bear Project researchers had only been able to capture and collar one to three bears a year, counting them was taking a long time. The researchers realized they needed a better way to check the population. They also wanted to know how many were males or females. How could they find this out?

BIG HAIRY DEAL

Native Mongolian bear researcher Odbayar (or Odko) Tumendemberel worked with the Gobi Bear Project to study Gobi bear DNA (genetic material). Her goal was to find out how closely these bears were related to grizzlies. The bear DNA would also reveal the data the Gobi Bear Project needed: how many bears there were, and how many males and females were in the population. Odko said, "I just needed a way to get some DNA to analyze from the different bears."

Odko's adviser for this work, Michael Proctor, worked with her to develop a strategy. The Gobi Bear Project team drove fence posts into the ground around each feeding station. Next, they strung barbed wire between the fence posts. If they were lucky, as the bears visited the feeding stations, the barbed wire would snatch a little bit of the animal's hair—a great source of DNA.

To go to the feeding station, Gobi bears had to duck under or jump over the barbed wire. The barbs snatched a bit of the bear's hair. Because their fuzzy coats are so thick, the barbs didn't hurt them.

Throughout 2008 and 2009, the barbed wire collected nearly one thousand hair samples. Odko analyzed them. First, she eliminated samples from repeat visitors to the feeding stations. Next, she compared Gobi bear DNA to the DNA from grizzlies and other brown bears.

Odko said, "I learned Gobi bears are genetically different from grizzlies—in fact, from all other bears. It made me believe it is important to save something so rare and so different."

Odko's genetic research revealed more information about the Gobi bear population that surprised everyone with the Gobi Bear Project.

Michael Proctor and Odko Tumendemberel collect a Gobi bear hair sample from the barbed-wire fence.

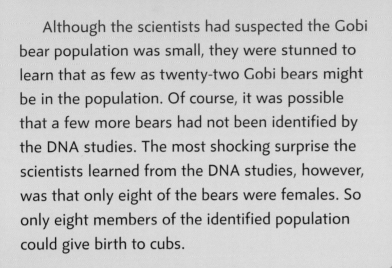

Although the scientists had suspected the Gobi bear population was small, they were stunned to learn that as few as twenty-two Gobi bears might be in the population. Of course, it was possible that a few more bears had not been identified by the DNA studies. The most shocking surprise the scientists learned from the DNA studies, however, was that only eight of the bears were females. So only eight members of the identified population could give birth to cubs.

With very few females in the population, it was important that each one be able to keep having cubs.

To focus more attention on the plight of the Gobi bears, Mongolian president Elbegdorj signed a proclamation to recognize 2013 as the Year of Protecting the Gobi Bear. Mongolia became the first nation in the world to officially designate the importance of protecting a bear of any species. Though most Mongolians—even people living near the GGSPA—would never see one of these rare bears, the year-long focus generated even more national support for Gobi bears.

Derek said, "The Gobi Bear Project produced a book about the bear for the children. The strongest conservation effort we could do for Gobi bears was to get the people to love them—[and then] lobby their own government to protect the bears."

In Mongolia, children in towns near the GGSPA learned about Gobi bears and how scientists are studying them using a GPS tracking collar.

Children (*above*) were inspired to form Gobi bear clubs to improve the habitat for the bears, promote recovery of the bear population, and raise funds to help buy food for the bear-feeding stations.

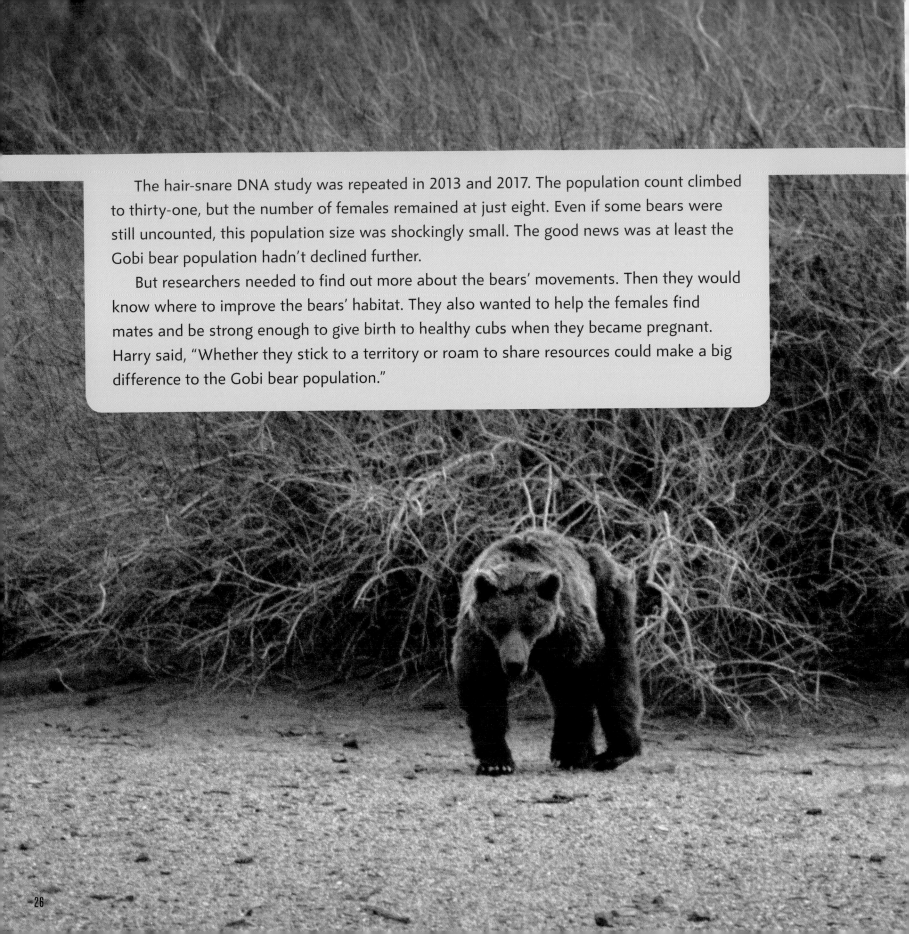

The hair-snare DNA study was repeated in 2013 and 2017. The population count climbed to thirty-one, but the number of females remained at just eight. Even if some bears were still uncounted, this population size was shockingly small. The good news was at least the Gobi bear population hadn't declined further.

But researchers needed to find out more about the bears' movements. Then they would know where to improve the bears' habitat. They also wanted to help the females find mates and be strong enough to give birth to healthy cubs when they became pregnant. Harry said, "Whether they stick to a territory or roam to share resources could make a big difference to the Gobi bear population."

WHERE'S THE BEAR?

Data was slowly coming in from the collared bears. Harry and the Gobi Bear Project team captured twenty-six different bears from 2005 through 2019, but fourteen were captured more than once. The Gobi Bear Project team began to piece together how individual bears were using their home ranges and how they were interacting with other bears. The bear that Harry had named Mother was recorded covering a 1,300-square-mile (3,370 sq. km) home range.

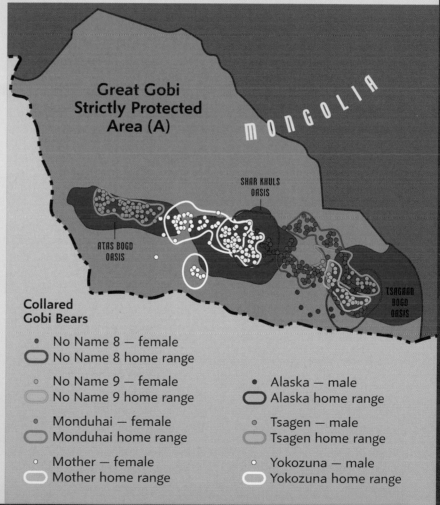

Great Gobi
Strictly Protected
Area (A)

MONGOLIA

SHAR KHULS
OASIS

ATAS BOGD
OASIS

TSAGAAN
BOGD
OASIS

**Collared
Gobi Bears**

- No Name 8 — female
- No Name 8 home range

- No Name 9 — female
- No Name 9 home range

- Monduhai — female
- Monduhai home range

- Mother — female
- Mother home range

- Alaska — male
- Alaska home range

- Tsagen — male
- Tsagen home range

- Yokozuna — male
- Yokozuna home range

In this copy of one of the Gobi Bear Project's tracking maps, each bear's range is shown outlined in a different color. The dots within each range mark that bear's GPS collar reported locations.

The team had also set up cameras at the feeding stations, which provided even more insight into Gobi bear behavior. One male Gobi bear was photographed at feeding stations near all three of the main oases. That was proof he was roaming across other bears' ranges rather than sticking to one area. Perhaps he was searching for mates.

Very few males that were photographed or captured had scars or other injuries. The Gobi Bear Project team believed this was evidence that Gobi bears were willing to share their home ranges.

Michael said, "Best, we got pictures of mothers with offspring—sometimes with yearlings, two-year-olds, or even three-year-olds." This gave the researchers hope the Gobi bear population was at least stable.

Armed with a better understanding of the long-term movements made by the bears, the Gobi Bear Project team decided to focus on improving areas close to the three main oases. To do this, they began working with a couple of new partners.

Look closely at the feeding station behind the bear. Food is put in the top of the box and rolls down into a feeding trough.

Scientists were pleased to see that the male snapped at three different locations looked strong and healthy.

SUPPLYING FOOD AND WATER

In 2017 Great Green Partners joined forces with Food for Mazaalai (the Mongolian word for Gobi bear). Great Green Partners is an international program for reclaiming and restoring deserts, and Food for Mazaalai is a Mongolian conservation group. Working together, they raised seedlings of the Gobi bear's favorite foods.

To get started, the groups collected seeds from native plants in the GGSPA, such as wild rhubarb and nitre bushes. Next, they analyzed the soil from the desert and created potting soil to match it. That way, when transplanted into the desert, the seedlings would have the best possible chance of surviving.

The seedlings for the Food for Mazaalai project are started in a greenhouse until they are ready to be planted. Meanwhile, local farmers in China are also raising plants that will be used to help restore plant life in the Gobi Desert.

Janet Hawkes, agricultural expert and consultant to the project, said, "The site choice for planting the seedlings must be chosen very carefully. We'll be planting an entire landscape—thousands of plants—all at once. And it'll be a walk-away planting, meaning we'll be leaving the seedlings to make it on their own." No one would come back to water the seedlings.

The project had a lot of volunteer support from the small towns edging the GGSPA(A), near an area used by the Gobi bears. The townspeople were mainly goat and camel herders who might want to let their animals graze in the planted areas. But the Food for Mazaalai team hoped that by helping the bears, the townspeople would want to save the food plants for the bears and graze their animals elsewhere.

Of course, the plants would still need time to grow up, drop seeds, and multiply to provide an ongoing food supply for the bears. Meanwhile, the feeding stations would continue to be restocked, since they were an important food source.

Since camels and gazelles prefer to graze on flatlands in the valleys, they eat most of the plants that are available there, leaving little for the bears. That means plants growing on a slope are more likely to remain untouched and become food for the bears.

Some oases, like this one, are a very small water source.

As climate change heats up the Gobi Desert, reliable water sources for the Gobi bears are at risk. The underground water table may shrink to the point of completely drying up some oases. Worse, the remaining water sources are already sometimes so small that they're spoiled by thirsty hooved animals, such as camels and gazelles, trampling the water into mud.

Harry said, "I believe global climate change and resulting droughts of water to be the biggest threat facing all the animals in the Gobi Desert."

The Mongolian government has made it a conservation priority to protect the existing water sources in the GGSPA. At one oasis, the spring water supplying it is piped into a cement trough. Though this is only about 6 feet (2 m) by 2.5 feet (0.7 m), it keeps the available water clear and drinkable. Hooved animals can't trample it into mud.

As if the environment doesn't already provide enough challenges, there is a new threat to Gobi bears invading the GGSPA, and it's often threatening them at the key oasis sites.

ENTER THE NINJA MINERS

Mongolia has what may be one of Earth's largest gold deposits. Gold has been known to exist in Mongolia since ancient times, but major commercial mining operations didn't begin until 1995. The first mining operation in the Gobi Desert started mining gold in 2013.

Some of that gold can be found within the GGSPA. So far, the Mongolian government has turned down requests by international companies to build roads and mines in the protected area. But that hasn't stopped illegal mining. These illegal miners are known as *ninja miners* in Mongolia. Though only individuals or small groups have invaded the GGSPA, the illegal miners often camp at the oases the bears depend on because water supplies are scarce.

The Mongolian government reports that rangers patrolling the GGSPA have caught as many as one hundred illegal miners in a year. Officially, the number of illegal miners is declining, but the motivation to search for gold remains. Most ninja miners are poor and willing to risk being caught so they can provide for their families.

Illegal miners dig holes to mine for gold in the GGSPA.

Ninja miners use picks and shovels to dig holes in the ground. The digging and scraping kills plants that could feed the desert animals, including Gobi bears. And when the ninja miners camp at the oases, they displace any nearby Gobi bears because the animals avoid people. When a bear can't get access to an oasis, it will have to trek on to the next one. Bears learn where to find the next closest oasis from following their mothers as cubs, but the next closest oasis is likely to be as much as 62 miles (100 km) away.

What will happen to the thirsty female Gobi bear that found people blocking her access to the oasis?

Once abandoned, the holes the miners dig become dangerous traps for the desert animals. According to herders in the area, drinking water that collects in these holes makes animals sick.

WHAT HAPPENS NEXT?

The female Gobi bear stands still, watching the group of people hurry away and climb into a big, lumpy, shiny thing—a van. The bear still hesitates after they disappear from view. The water scent, however, continues to draw her until she can no longer resist. She plods over to the water-filled trough for a drink. Lifting her dripping muzzle, she huffs throaty grunts.

Watching through their van's windows, the people the female feared—Gobi bear researchers—exchange smiles. Through the window they watch a fuzzy Gobi cub burst out of tall grass. It trots fast to reach its mother and drink alongside her.

The cub is living proof that efforts to make a difference for the Gobi bear population are helping. Harry said, "Continuing to give these bears a chance—that's what we're after."

An energetic Gobi bear cub is a good sign it's healthy.

Polar Bears Need Help Too

Polar bears are also perfectly adapted to live and find food in their harsh home environment—the Arctic. But, as of the last survey in 2015, polar bears are listed as vulnerable on the IUCN Red List. While scientists estimate that as many as thirty-one thousand polar bears remain, scientists don't know how many bears are needed for a healthy population. Worse, the population is shrinking.

Polar bears depend on using floating sheets of sea ice as a hunting platform for catching prey, such as seals. Rising temperatures due to climate change mean the ice is melting earlier and forming later each year. So polar bears have less prime hunting time, which means they may not build up the needed fat reserve to survive when there's too much open water for them to easily catch prey. If this climate change continues, the polar bear population, like the Gobi bear population, will struggle to survive.

Measuring as much as 8 feet (2.4 m) long and weighing around 1,400 pounds (635 kg), adult polar bears are one of the biggest meat eaters on Earth.

Author's Note

I want to share my research journey to telling the Gobi bear rescue story. It started with a TV program mentioning that these unique, desert-living bears were critically endangered. *Bears living in a desert and now they're rare*—I had to know more!

I first tracked down and interviewed bear biologists Harry Reynolds and Derek Craighead. They had each spent decades studying grizzly bears and wanted to help the Gobi bears. So they were spending part of each year in Mongolia, camping out in the Gobi Desert while working to understand this bear's life enough to help the population remain stable—and hopefully find a way to enable it to increase.

This is where the unfolding story really became exciting. I Skyped around the world to interview Michael Proctor, Odko Tumendemberel, and Janet Hawkes. These experts kindly shared their work and efforts for the bears, their deep concern for the animals came through along with a driving sense of urgency that was contagious. But the most recent population survey was inspiring hope.

Then, like a movie, where just as things are looking up something terrible happens, I learned of the newest blow to the bears' chance for survival—GOLD and the efforts of big mining companies to access deposits in the Gobi Desert. The Mongolian government is, so far, favoring protecting the bears over the opportunity to share in big mining profits. Mongolia deserves worldwide applause for making this choice.

I end this rescue story hopeful for the Gobi bear's future. That hope has been hard earned by an international team of researchers and determined local scientists and citizens. Only time will tell if the hope becomes reality.

Timeline

1943 Scientists confirm bears live in the Gobi Desert, though native people were aware of their existence.

1953 Hunting of the Gobi bear is banned by the Mongolian government.

1976 The Great Gobi Strictly Protected Area is established to give Gobi bears and other animals a safe habitat with access to food and water.

1987 The Gobi bear is first listed as very rare in the Mongolian Red Book of protected animals. Since it hasn't been officially classified, it isn't on the IUCN Red List.

1990 The GGSPA is made a biosphere reserve by the United Nations Educational, Scientific and Cultural Organization. This further protects the GGSPA for research and conservation.

1992 The Mongolian government establishes feeding stations to supplement the Gobi bear food supply.

1992–2014 Germanwatch's Global Climate Risk Index, issued in 2014, listed Mongolia among the top ten countries affected by extreme weather events during this period. Besides drought, these events included extremely low temperatures following heavy rainfalls, which causes ice to cover plants that are food sources.

1993–2007 Drought dropped average rainfall from 3.9 inches (10 cm) per year to 1.9 inches (5 cm) per year.

2000 The Gobi bear is listed under the Mongolian Law on Fauna as critically endangered. It is also listed under the Convention on International Trade in Endangered Species of Wild Fauna and Flora (CITES) as very rare and protected.

2005 The Gobi Bear Project researchers begin putting tracking collars on Gobi bears to help the Mongolian government protect them.

Cameras are set up to estimate the population size. The first photo of a Gobi bear is taken by Harry Reynolds.

2008–2009 Genetic analysis of one thousand Gobi bear hair samples is used to estimate minimum population size and number of male and female bears. Fourteen males and eight females are found.

2013 Mongolia names 2013 the Year of Protecting the Gobi Bear as a plea for the world to join them in protecting them.

The first gold mining operation in the Gobi Desert began.

2018 A three-year project to supply technical assistance for Gobi bear conservation is launched jointly by the governments of Mongolia and China. This includes setting up 150 infrared automatic cameras in GGSPA to monitor Gobi bear movements among parts of the desert in each country.

What is one thing you would like to be able to add to this timeline in the future?

Glossary

climate change: major long-term changes in expected weather patterns

critically endangered: a species facing an extremely high risk of extinction

cub: a young bear

desert: an area with an annual rainfall of less than 9.8 inches (25 cm)

drought: a long period without rain

ecosystem: a community of animals that interact within a natural environment

ecotype: an animal uniquely adapted to survive in its environment

endangered: a species facing a high risk of extinction

extinct: a species that no longer has any living members

habitat: natural home environment of a plant or an animal

hibernate: to spend a season in an inactive state, almost like sleeping, but in which the animal's temperature and heart rate are much reduced

instinct: something an animal is able to do without being taught

mazaalai: the Mongolian word for Gobi bear

oasis: an area in a desert where water is found

species: one kind of living thing

umbrella species: a species that has the same needs as many other species in that ecosystem. When an umbrella species is protected, many other species within that habitat are protected too.

vulnerable: a species that is close to being endangered

Source Notes

8   Harry Reynolds, interview with the author, October 28, 2018 and May 15, 2019.

14   Derek Craighead, interview with the author, October 11, 2018.

17   Reynolds, interview.

21   Reynolds.

22   Odbayar Tumendemberel, interview with the author, October 28, 2018.

23   Tumendemberel.

25   Craighead, interview.

26   Reynolds, interview.

28   Michael Proctor, interview with the author, October 15, 2018.

30   Janet Hawkes, interview with the author, May 2, 2019.

31   Reynolds, interview.

34   Reynolds.

Find Out More

Clarke, Ginjer L. *What's Up in the Gobi Desert?* New York: Grosset & Dunlap, 2016.
Dig even deeper into the ways the Gobi Desert is unlike other deserts.

Gobi Bear Project
https://www.gobibearproject.org
Explore this site to see more photos of Gobi bears and learn more about the ongoing work being done to help them.

Gobi Desert Facts & Information
https://gobidesert.org/
Find out more about the animals, climate, and people of the Gobi Desert.

National Geographic. *National Geographic Readers: Bears*. Washington, DC: National Geographic, 2016.
Learn about different kinds of bears in this photo-filled book.

"Saving the World's Rarest Bears." National Geographic video, 5:21.
https://video.nationalgeographic.com/video/news/00000145-6c9a-de1f-a1fd-6c9efbae0000.
This video brings Gobi bears and their amazing home habitat to life.

Index

Photo Acknowledgments

Image credits: Joe Riis, pp. 1, 4, 8 (both), 13, 14, 15, 17, 19, 20 (top), 22, 23, 25 (both), 28 (bottom), 30, 31, 34; Laura Westlund/Independent Picture Service, pp. 6, 11, 20 (bottom), 27; LightRocket/Getty Images, p. 7; Timothy Allen/Getty Images, p. 9; Eric Dragesco/naturepl.com, pp. 10, 26; Natthawat/Getty Images, p. 12; Dr. Harry Reynolds/Gobi Bear Project, pp. 16, 18, 21, 28 (top); Joel Bennett/Getty Images, p. 24; Zhang Meng/Xinhua News Agency/Newscom, p. 29; Tomohiro Ohsumi/Bloomberg/Getty Images, pp. 32, 33; Wolfgang Kaehler/LightRocket/Getty Images, p. 35; supanut piyakanont/Getty Images (plant graphic).

Cover image: Joe Riis; supanut piyakanont/iStock/Getty Images; Nayuki/Moment/Getty Images.